To all my teachers, especially Les, Marg and Rinpoche.
Also to heart dwellers John, Ken, Steph, Pen, and Em. – L.B.

To Nonna, Nonno, and Zio, my brighter stars – A.P.

Text copyright © 2018 Louise Bladen
Illustrations copyright © 2018 Angela Perrini
First published in Australia in 2018 by Little Steps Publishing
48 Ross St. Glebe NSW 2037
Translation rights licensed through Alc Agency

Published in 2020 by Beaming Books, an imprint of 1517 Media.

25 24 23 22 21 20        2 3 4 5 6 7 8

ISBN: 978-1-5064-6377-3

Library of Congress Control Number: 2019949292

65087; 9781506454009; FEB2020

Beaming Books
510 Marquette Avenue
Minneapolis, MN 55402
Beamingbooks.com

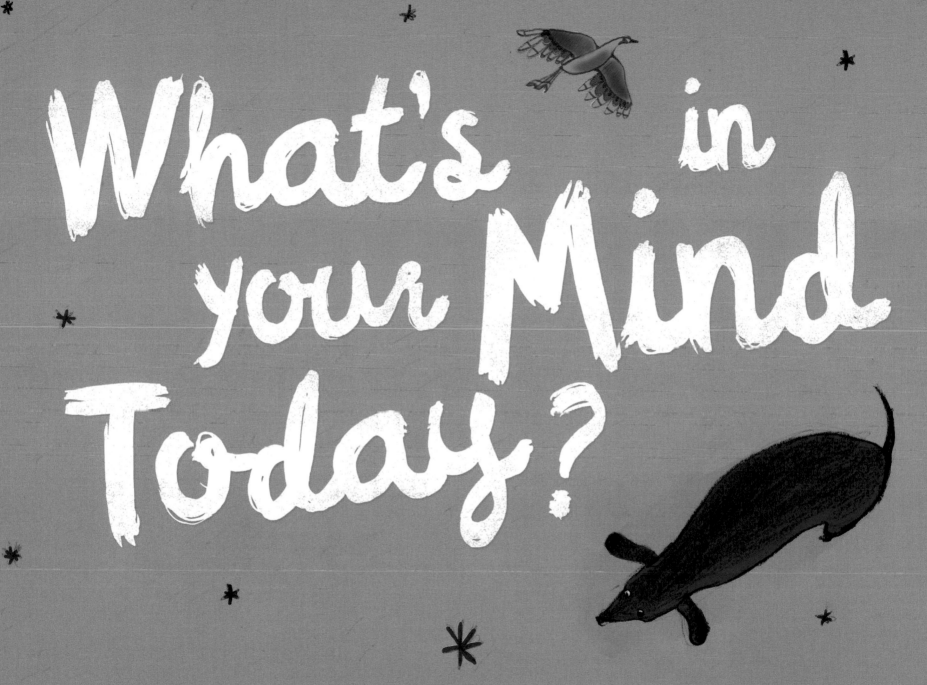

# What's in your Mind Today?

written by
Louise Bladen

beaming books
MINNEAPOLIS

illustrated by
ANGELA PERRINI

# What's in your mind today?

Let's see what's there, hiding inside.
Sit very still and close your eyes.

Take a deep breath **in** . . . and **out** it goes.
Can you feel the air rushing through your nose?

Counting your breaths can be such fun.

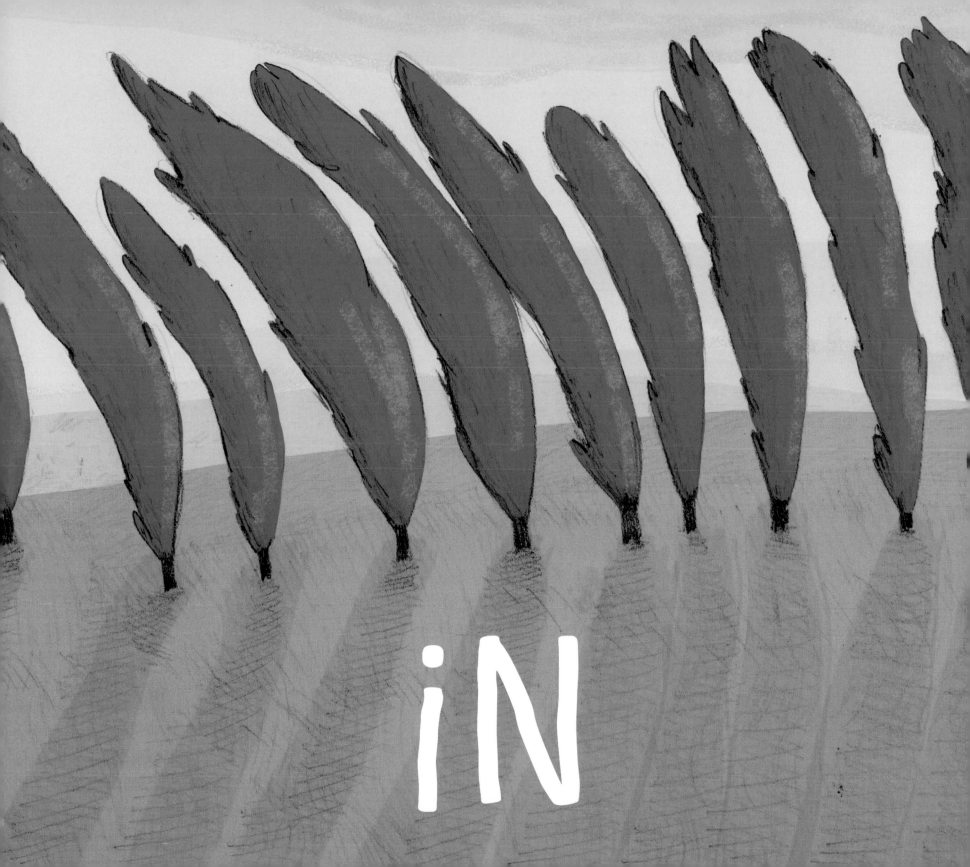

and then OUT and that is one.

**In** and **out** again, you're up to two.
Now there are only eight more to do.
**In** . . . and **out** . . . and there goes three.

There's lots of air in
your lungs, you see.

Now there's four,
then five goes past.
Some are slow and
some are fast.

Count every breath,
right up to ten,
then you can open
your eyes again.

Now take a look
at the thoughts
in your mind.
Are they angry or
are they kind?

Molly's thoughts are butterflies.
They *flit* and *flutter*
all over the skies.

She can't catch them,
she's too slow.
Where do they come from,
where do they go?

Oliver's thoughts are monsters,
*stomping* around.
Their great big feet
are shaking the ground.

But when he looks at them
they just melt away.
They have no power
of their own to stay.

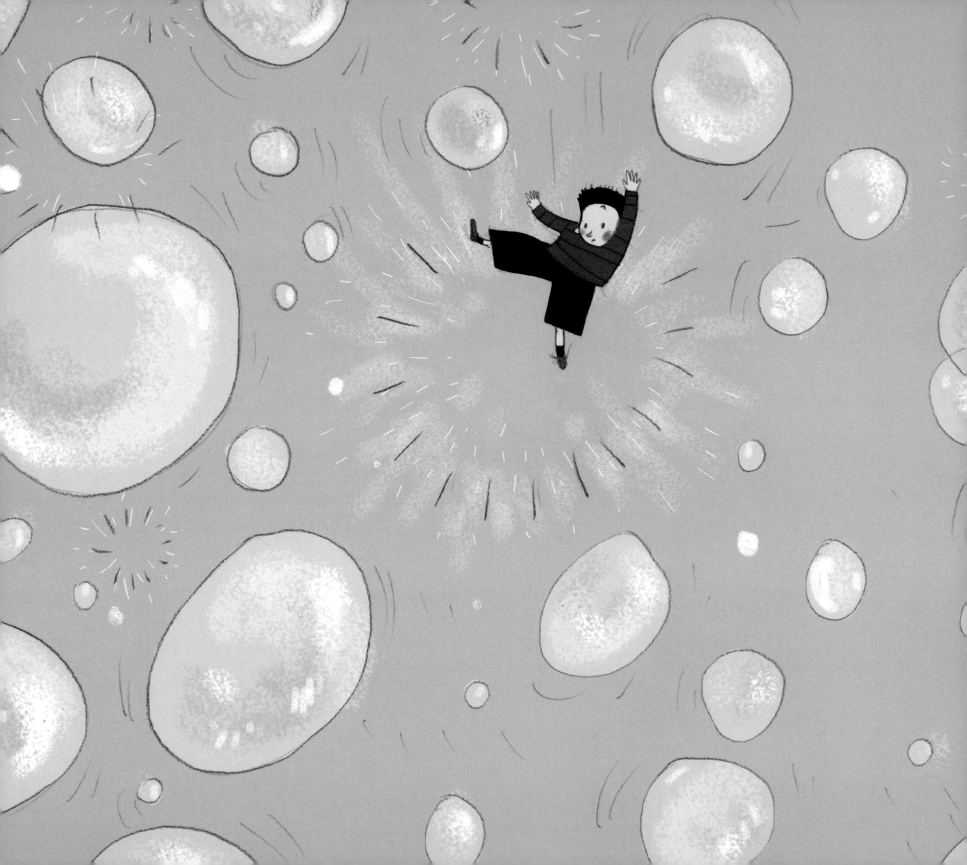

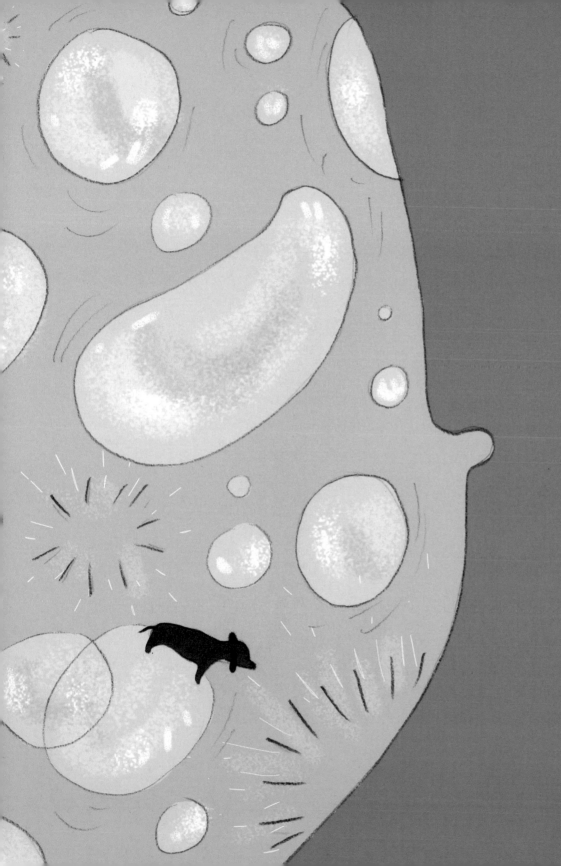

George's thoughts are
full of troubles,
*boiling* and *bursting*
in great big bubbles.

With his mind
he makes them *pop*.
Oh, what fun!
But why did they stop?

Amelia's thoughts are
*wriggly* worms,
wobbling around
to make her squirm.

"Wriggle away," she says,
"you don't worry me."
Where have they gone now?
There's nothing to see!

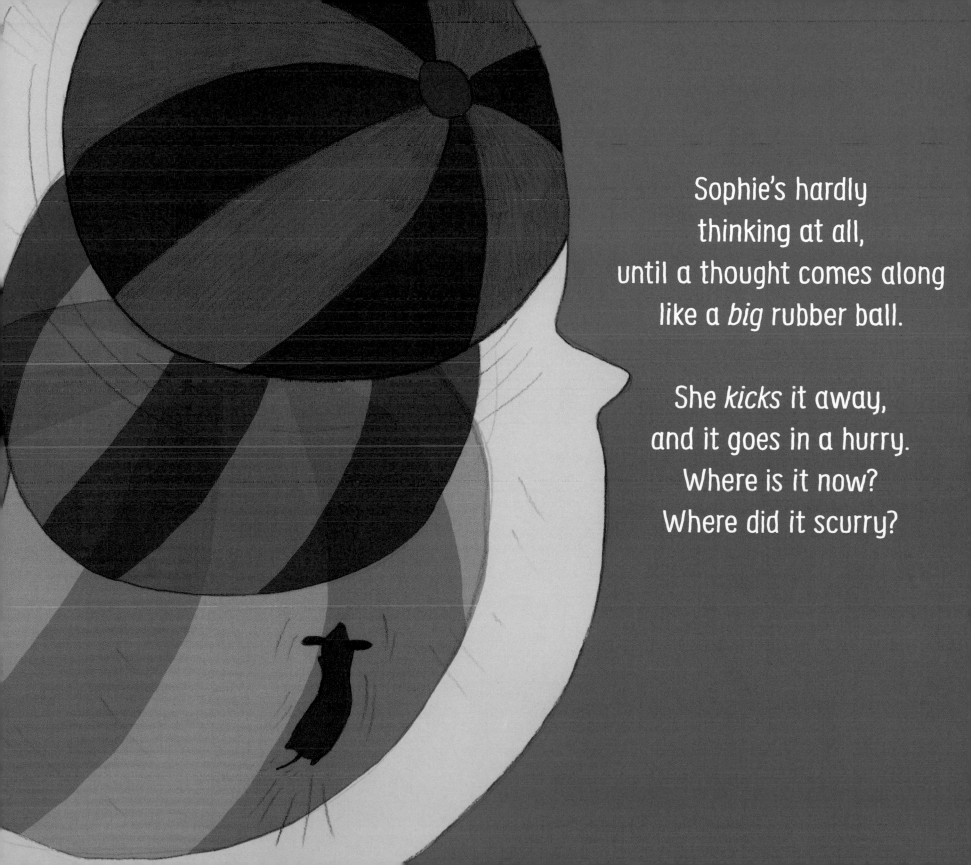

Sophie's hardly
thinking at all,
until a thought comes along
like a *big* rubber ball.

She *kicks* it away,
and it goes in a hurry.
Where is it now?
Where did it scurry?

So what's in your mind?
Are your thoughts good or bad?
Are they making you happy
or making you sad?

Good or bad, remember that thoughts never last.
Sooner or later, even scary thoughts pass.

Thoughts are a little like clouds, you see.
They come and they go, blown on the breeze.

Just finding your breath can put you at ease.
Watch your thoughts drift away, then feel calm . . .

. . . and at peace.